Christopher Columbus

by Mary Dodson Wade

Content Consultant

Nanci R. Vargus, Ed.D.
Professor Emeritus, University of Indianapolis

Reading Consultant

Jeanne Clidas, Ph.D.
Reading Specialist

Children's Press®
An Imprint of Scholastic Inc.
New York Toronto London Auckland Sydney
Mexico City New Delhi Hong Kong
Danbury, Connecticut

Library of Congress Cataloging-in-Publication Data
Wade, Mary Dodson.
 Christopher Columbus/by Mary Dodson Wade; poem by Jodie Shepherd. — [Revised edition with new text and illustrations].
     pages cm. — (Rookie biographies)
 Includes bibliographical references and index.
 ISBN 978-0-531-20559-4 (library binding: alk. paper) — ISBN 978-0-531-21202-8 (pbk.: alk. paper)
  1. Columbus, Christopher--Juvenile literature. 2. Explorers—America—Biography—Juvenile literature. 3. Explorers—Spain—Biography—Juvenile literature. 4. America—Discovery and exploration—Spanish—Juvenile literature. I. Shepherd, Jodie. II. Title.

E111.W24 2014
970.01'5092—dc23 [B]   2014014824

Produced by Spooky Cheetah Press
Poem by Jodie Shepherd
Design by Keith Plechaty

© 2015 by Scholastic Inc.

Printed in China 62

SCHOLASTIC, CHILDREN'S PRESS, ROOKIE BIOGRAPHIES®, and associated logos are trademarks and/or registered trademarks of Scholastic Inc.

1 2 3 4 5 6 7 8 9 10 R 24 23 22 21 20 19 18 17 16 15

Photographs ©: Alamy Images/Archive Images: cover; AP Images: 12, 15 (North Wind Picture Archives), 3 top left; Getty Images: 27 (Erika Santelices/AFP), 23 (Stock Montage), 31 bottom (Visions of America/UIG); iStockphoto/kickstand: 28, 30 top right; Media Bakery/Visions of America: 3 bottom, 31 top; Superstock, Inc.: 3 top right (Nikhilesh Haval/age fotostock), 4, 30 top left; The Image Works: 24, 31 center bottom (akg-images), 20 (J. Bedmar/Iberfoto), 16 (Lee Snider), 11, 31 center top (North Wind Picture Archives); Thinkstock/Peter Dennis: 8.

Maps by XNR Productions, Inc.: 7, 19

Table of Contents

Meet Christopher Columbus

Christopher Columbus was an **explorer** who lived in Europe. During his lifetime, people in Europe did not know about North or South America. In 1492, Columbus had the idea to sail to China. He landed in the Americas instead!

Columbus was born in Genoa in 1451. The tall, red-haired boy did not want to be a weaver like his father. He became a sailor.

Columbus was born in Genoa.

A Sailor's Life

In Columbus's time, people traveled by ship to buy and sell goods in faraway lands. Many countries in Europe wanted to trade with China, Japan, and India. Those countries were in an area called the East Indies. The trip was long and dangerous.

Columbus studied the different ways to get from Europe to the East Indies.

Columbus learned how waves and wind move ships on the water. He studied the stars and used them to **navigate**. Columbus could tell where he was by looking at the stars, even when he was on the ocean!

Hundreds of years ago, sailors used the stars to navigate.

11

When he was 25 years old, Columbus worked on a ship. When pirates attacked the ship, Columbus escaped by swimming to Portugal. Soon after his arrival, Columbus got married and had a son named Diego. During this time, Columbus studied maps and books to find a shorter, safer way to reach China from Europe.

Into the Unknown

Columbus thought he found a better route to China. He needed a ship to test his plan. The King of Portugal would not give him money. Later, Columbus went to Spain. After six years, King Ferdinand and Queen Isabella of Spain agreed to pay for his trip.

Columbus shares his plan with the King and Queen of Spain.

On August 3, 1492, Columbus set out with three ships: the *Niña*, the *Pinta*, and the *Santa Maria*. After being on the ocean for 30 days, the sailors became afraid. They had never gone that long without seeing land.

FAST FACT!

The *Santa Maria* was the largest of Columbus's ships, but the *Niña* was his favorite. He sailed it to America three times.

As more days went by, the sailors were ready to **rebel**. Then, on October 12, 1492, someone shouted, "Land!" Columbus stopped at San Salvador, near Cuba. Friendly Taino people lived there. Columbus was sure he was near China.

FAST FACT!

Today, we celebrate Columbus Day on the second Monday in October.

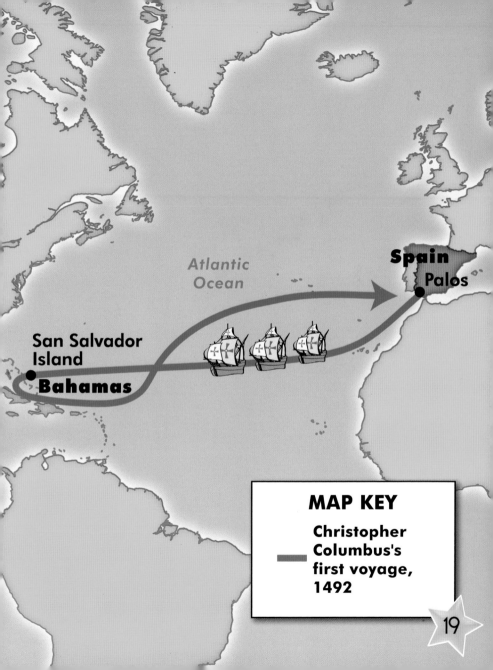

Atlantic
Ocean

San Salvador
Island

Bahamas

Spain
Palos

MAP KEY

Christopher Columbus's first voyage, 1492

Columbus explored the islands. He did not see the great riches he had been expecting. In fact, the Taino people were poor. Columbus was sure he would still find riches. And now he knew he could sail west and find land. He hurried home to tell everyone he had been to the East Indies.

Columbus thought he had landed in the East Indies. He called the people he met "Indians."

A New World

When Columbus returned to Spain, he was a hero. He planned a second trip. This time he was to bring settlers and animals to the islands. Many people wanted to accompany Columbus on his second voyage, in 1493.

Columbus brought home corn, chili peppers, and parrots. People in Europe had never seen these things.

23

When settlers did not find the riches they expected, they blamed Columbus. Columbus went back to Spain to explain. When he returned to the island a third time, angry settlers had him arrested and sent him back to Spain.

FAST FACT!

When Europeans arrived in the New World, they brought diseases that the natives had never experienced before. Many of the Taino later died from these diseases.

Columbus made a fourth voyage, in 1502. He had bad luck. His ships fell apart. He was **stranded** on an island for almost a year. Columbus finally got back to Spain but died not long after that. He was 55 years old.

No one knows exactly where Columbus is buried. Some people think his body rests inside this structure in the Dominican Republic.

Timeline of Christopher Columbus's Life

1492
makes first voyage to America

1451
born in Genoa

1493
makes second voyage with large fleet

Christopher Columbus was not successful in discovering a new route to China. However, he was the first European to visit what would become known as the Americas. Columbus was a daring explorer. His travels changed what people knew about the world.

1498
ends third voyage as a prisoner

1506
dies on May 20

1502
makes fourth voyage to America

A Poem About Christopher Columbus

In 1492, Columbus had the notion

he'd reach a foreign country by sailing 'cross the ocean.

The sea was deep and wide; the trip was hard and slow.

But finally, success! A sailor called, "Land ho!"

You Can Be Adventurous

- Read books to learn about new places, cultures, and customs.

- Do not be afraid to try new things that interest you.

Glossary

explorer (ek-SPLOR-ur): someone who travels to discover what a place is like

navigate (NAV-uh-gate): travel using maps, compasses, and stars to guide you

rebel (ri-BEL): refuse to follow those in charge

stranded (STRAND-ed): left in a strange or unpleasant place with no way to leave

Index

Facts for Now

Visit this Scholastic Web site for more information
on Christopher Columbus:
www.factsfornow.scholastic.com
Enter the keywords **Christopher Columbus**

About the Author

Mary Dodson Wade loves to read, write books, and travel. She has been to China and to the East Indies (Indonesia), but she flew in an airplane. She saw wonderful things, and she brought back spices.